ONWARD TOWARD SALVATION
TESTIMONY

ONWARDS TOWARDS SALVATION

Copyright © 2024 Redmond Holt

Paperback ISBN: 978-1-915223-37-1

All rights reserved.

No part of this publication may be reproduced, stored in a retrieval system, or transmitted in any form or by any means, electronic, mechanical, photocopying or otherwise, without prior written consent of the publisher except as provided under United Kingdom copyright law. Short extracts may be used for review purposes with credits given.

Except in the case of historical fact, any resemblance to actual persons living or dead is purely coincidental.

Unless otherwise indicated, all scripture quotations are taken from the New King James Version® (NKJ®), © 2013 by Holman Bible Publishers. Nashville, Tennessee. Used by permission of Holman. All Rights Reserved.

Published by

Maurice Wylie Media
Your Inspirational & Christian Book Publisher

For more information visit
www.MauriceWylieMedia.com

Dedication

In memory of my friend Robert Rowen.

1933 – HOME

Contents

Introduction 9

Your reflections or message to loved ones

PART 1: ARE WE NOT ALL BARABBAS 11
- A life vain lived 13
- The odious stain of sin 15
- Guilty 18
- A quest for peace 19
- Underworld 22
- Self cast down 28
- The self serving prayer 30
- The last testimony of Pontius Pilate . . . 31

PART 2: A GREAT LIGHT SHONE FORTH 33
- Desperation cry 35
- Quickening 38
- His miracle brought forth 39
- The way, the truth and the life 41
- Damascus Sun 43
- I cost His Blood 45
- Atonement 47
- Guilt expunged 48
- Psalm 70 times 7 52
- In conversation 54
- His change wrought forth 56

PART 3: CONFIDENT AND ASSURRED 59
- What beauty 61
- His Name alone 63
- Hard truth 66
- Discernment 68
- Be ye not deceived 69
- Eternity 75
- The prayer 76
- Praise His Holy Name 77

About the Author 79

Introduction

All of us reside at some point across the spectrum of salvation. Some people just care for the passing pleasures of today while others greatly thirst for the peace and security of eternal salvation. Many place their trust in a tradition and practice routine to satisfy their gods. Jesus Christ tells us that we must be born again. That is to repent of our sins and to trust in the completed work of God's only begotten son; His death, burial and resurrection.

The Bible teaches that God our Father sent His Son Jesus to die for our sins and this He did on Calvary's cross. Jesus, raised from the dead on the third day, first appeared to many and then ascended to heaven where He sits at the Father's right hand. He left us His Spirit and today The Holy Spirit lives in the hearts of those who believe and trust in the atoning Blood of the Saviour; Jesus Christ the only mediator between God and humankind. While this is good news it is not a popular message: the Bible tells us that our salvation is a free gift of God's grace that we cannot earn by our performance, our good works or by paying for it with our money. We like to impart some measure of human input but Jesus has done it all. The ransom for your sin is paid in full by Him and Him alone.

My chief objective in writing this book is to encourage you to explore what Jesus Christ has done for you. I've traced the story of an "any person" and chart their pilgrimage from a life lived for themselves to the conclusion when they are worshipping God in eternity.

I would also encourage you to read God's Holy Word. Some of you do every day, some may be encouraged to lift the dusty pages from a book shelf and others of you may be encouraged enough to purchase your own copy. Regardless please know that God loves you and He places great value upon you and He is seriously concerned about your eternal destiny.

As the world quickens towards the culmination of all things I have enclosed the next page for you to capture your own thoughts and meditations. Some of you may also wish to write a message of encouragement and hope to a loved one.

I hope you enjoy reading this journey and that we will one day meet in the New Jerusalem. God bless you and your family.

Part 1

Are we not all Barabbas

A LIFE VAIN LIVED

Luke 12:16-20.

"Then He spoke a parable to them saying: "The ground of a certain rich man yielded plentifully. And he thought within himself, saying 'what shall I do since I have no room to store my crops?' So he said 'I will do this: I will pull down my barns and build greater, and there I will store all my crops and goods. And I will say to my soul, "Soul, you have many goods laid up for many years; take your ease; eat, drink and be merry." But God said to him, 'Fool! This night your soul will be required of you: then whose will those things be which you have provided?"

This life full vain lived I.
Tempted every sense with rigour pressed zeal,
toward vice with wild abandon I did flee,
nought held back with no regard for thee.
Full bead, brim thread, possessed by furious pace,
passion uncorked, all to touch, all to taste.

Confident projected voice demanding all the more,
conceited scheming manifested by thunder filled roar,
tumult compassed by ego, power and grasp for wealth,
pronouncing inconsiderate judgement with ease and stealth.
Conveying sentence, dispensing justice as I pleased,
securing continued advantage with haste and speed.

Barns built to roof up with riches high,
this here my world for I will never die.

By avarice I sought and coveted a golden calf,
plotting and carousing; no wish to compose my epitaph,
striking out and stealing from those poorer,
careful yet not to drink their cup of sorrow.

The taste of lips enjoying pleasure's lust filled hunger,
an untiring quest; lives uncaringly pulled asunder.
There was no cost to my black-hearted rage,
hunting, hounding this globe venturing every trail.
I did not yield, to all impulses I did agree,
full blooded, this zest for self came so easily.

It seemed like there was no consequences to charm and thrill,
ruling by fear and self-satisfied deceiving grin.
Caught unawares, beware what I did not want to hear,
man kills everything and what man does not kill......time will.

THE ODIOUS STAIN OF SIN

Romans 3:19-20.

"Now we know that whatever the law says, it says to those who are under the law, that every mouth may be stopped, and all the world may become guilty before God. Therefore by the deeds of the law no flesh will be justified in His sight, for by the law is the knowledge of sin."

This life full vain I ran with a curious pace,
self-centred gain my ego's ambition finding place.
Wealth, position, power my conniving wisdom did soon me bring,
I worked this heart of mine and made it sing.

I did one day awake to conscience roar,
this first enlightenment of hurt I tried ignore.
Remembrance of tears to friends I caused with pain,
becoming a stranger to those I love through contempt and disdain.

Weeks later red hot conscience called again,
thoughts rekindled, impure, causing embarrassment and shame.
Images of those I scorned, abused, slandered and deframed,
faces with flattering lips but in fear they all cursed my name.

Harangued, hounded, vexed; troubling thoughts pursued me,
every waking hour I did run but could not flee.
No peace found, I turned to pleasure flesh and glass decanter,
debasing myself again, hoping vice would buy me succour.

Surrender came: a cold morn collapsed I against chapel pew,
Preacher's call reciting words that I from childhood knew.
Confronted by God's law against which I could not stand,
one by one Decalogue's damnation painted eternity's demand.

The law of pounded truth my breath it made exhale,
"Repent" He cried; the cost His blood by nail.
His law of ten it tried me rip in two,
my memory burnt with vision of what He already knew.

Out of Egypt, He said He brought me home,
but my Babylonian heart could not worship Him alone.

No gods of idol stone He beckoned carve,
but I am my own god; it is only me I serve.

I made myself blush with tongue so black and vile,
cursing God and man raw with poisonous bile.

The Sabbath was my every day, for pleasure each hour I did crave.
I, a prodigy of satan, bought wanton acts of decay.

A plunderer of parents, their riches and their dreams.
Calculating, counting cunningly by any nefarious means.

You shall not murder but this I've done by times,
with tongue and thought death was hastened in my mind.

Adultery's lust: I've craved the touch of rich and poor,
destroying families without consideration; always yearning more.

Stolen treasures filled my barns full to bulging roof,
taken arbitrarily but what is worse, I also extinguished victim's hope.

False witness bore in court, in talk and deed.
I've shattered innocence, deceiving multitudes to serve my needs.

I covet all, I let no man nor fiend stand in way,
restitution required..........
No. I'd rather walk away.

His words cut quick, so many I did despise,
I held no fear of man or God afore my eyes.
This heart like Pharaoh hardened though the message did enthral,
I must submit myself to recklessness and avoid His justice call.

GUILTY

James 2:10.

*"For whoever shall keep the whole law and yet stumble in one point,
he is guilty of all."*

Weighed Deliberately.
In full consideration they carried a betrayer's kiss.
A plot: conspired in collusion to its deadly end.

Murderous.

With intent these hands have schemed; weaved.
They have played the instruments of war, both hate and mirth
and have not known the difference.

These same hands have delicately embraced,
conveying tender touch of loving gaze with a frenzy,
a fury of pace.

These hands that birthed innocence
have rent in two a purple shroud,
have hammered thorn and nail,
have clutched the spear of ill-informed choice.

Racked and plagued with conscience searing,
these hands cannot be bleached.

Broken, enraged, lined, toiled, frightened and trembling.

These hands are mine.

A QUEST FOR PEACE

Ecclesiastes 1:13-14.

"And I set my heart to seek and search out by wisdom concerning all that is done under heaven; this burdensome task God has given to the sons of man, by which they may be exercised.
I have seen all the works that are done under the sun: and indeed, all is vanity and grasping for the wind."

Hope expunged
death knell toll
mark of Cain
scars my Soul.
No escape
no victory
prosecution arraigned;
pronounced guilty.
Fate is set
I cannot flee,
Abel's blood
spilt on me.

Searched for peace
I could not find
travelled far
journeyed wide.
By force of hand
I worked
I toiled,
on mountain high
in deep cut mine,
I dug at holes

and mended ditches
lumbered wood
built brick bridges,
ploughed in fields
saw cities of cranes,
where 'ere I looked
death called my name.

Gold accrued
wages spent
mammon escapes
all circumstance.
I killed for coin
spent it fast
robbed and pillaged
it did not last.
Tasted pleasure
wines and drug
gorged at food
harlot's hugs.
Bulging wallet
fickle friend
found alone
at money's end.

Built a god
of rounded stone
brushed and sanded
soft smooth curve.
Standing sentinel
golden calf
conscience sated
peace at last.
Travel companion
placed in bag
worshiped at night
by candle light.

To it I kneel
with scraping bow
all answers found
at witching hour.
One day it fell
smote to crust,
smashing ground
now fine dust.
For peace I ventured
to follow man,
vain traditions
in every land.
Long black cloaks
hats of red,
incense smoke
crozier choke.
Others follow
deluded men
marching in circles
and around again.
Wise men, fools
creeping things,
moon gods, sun gods,
plants and trees.
Give me money
send you a cure
make me rich
you stay poor.
Brood of vipers
hornet's nest,
hypocrite demons
motives unchecked.

Sets of rules
bars set high,
such hard work
I'd rather die!

UNDERWORLD – A VISION OF HELL

John 8:23-24

"And He said to them, "you are from beneath; I am from above.
You are of this world; I am not of this world.
Therefore I said to you that you will die in your sins;
for if you do not believe that I am He, you will die in your sins."

Overcome.
Suffocating.
Last gasp rasp wheeze of broken air
then death rattle:
life suddenly extinguished.
With wrestled breath
my spirit fled this mortal coil.
To death surrendered I
with feral fight and perished howl,
my bounty of youth and wealth dispersed like vapour:
all vanished.
With a last eye flicker
of conscious thought,
I to darkened depths
downward plunged.

Unrelenting.
Defiled and debauched,
this was no merge to promised abyss.
Flailing limbs to jaws open wide,
a dark pit
to which I did slide.
My spotted soul,

unclean,
took residence
midst the sinful shores of Sheol.
This Hades
of scorch scream,
depressed and bleak black,
a pillared pit of souls abandoned.
Pungent sulphur;
clawing, gnawing despair.
Repent they had exhorted
to which I had laughed,
you cannot have forgiveness
for what you do not believe.
My reward now applied malevolently;
I translated quickly
with haste bent fury,
disgorged speedily to cavern home.
Immediate, sudden and foreboding,
no escape;
lost, forlorn.

Three days hence
through shadowed mist
my funeral pyre I spied.
Mourners gathered
comforting each other in blissful ignorance,
plying clamorous platitudes
to those I yearned to warn.
Regret and tears shed I
for they me soon by time will join.
In their forever halls
of stone idol, iron, clay
came earnest prayer of plea,
mingled with the rise of incense smoke
their repeated Calvary sacrifices,
fabricated by blood soaked hand

were again eaten to no avail.
Black clad cloaks,
assuaged their guilt,
but all in vain for me.
My mortal remains raised to shoulder high,
to scratch deep grave
coldly depositing my redundant frame
afore my memory was toasted
then lost to warmed decanted vines.

This Abaddon pit,
domain of Hell
I slotted like chattel
in Gehenna's cell.
Full presence felt I
though all thought pulled asunder,
the full extraction for my sin
pelt mercilessly across my soul.
This ceaseless crucifixion
this unyielding hammer of spear and steel
accompanied by darkened voices
noisily approaching, growling,
breathing slow then to disappear.
Some taking last battle stand were tortured
they I from distance heard;
their blood whipped roars
mixed with the manic mumblings of demons
pressed, wrestling together against chain clank floor.
In my midst my senses heightened,
made ready for gaolers prod and goad
for full measure of fear is the currency of punishment.

From the parable of olden script
searched I for the Richman and Lazarus.
Across the visible divide and impregnable chasm

Abraham's Bosom empty I did spy;
The Son of Man had from Paradise
delivered His Blood bought ransomed,
they now co-heirs with He who rose from dead.
The still un-named Richman wailed in anguished tempest,
he long since joined by perdition bound kin,
they mourning in fear and trembling,
lips still parched for soothing balm.
Shielded by fierce pitch darkness,
burning thirst and mounting heat,
no quench for scraping broken hands.

Nephelim of the netherworld awaited their master,
he whose reign would soon be over,
no peace promised at his fiendish end.
The world's Potentate of theft and murder,
this wretched Ambassador of vice and wicked deceit
was cast unceremoniously with vengeance rigour;
accompanied by falsehood prophet,
seen they then for worthless spine.
All us dead loosed upon him with murderous rage
with one intent; his again demise.
Diabolical savagery hence uninvented
we cast upon this heathen despotic
with words and terror we brought he to near slaughter
we now stuck forever in this his infernal hereafter.
Contorted heathen,
monstrous jowls,
stench breath sewer
lost, never found.

Some time then, a distant trumpet call.
I saw the righteous in heartbeat caught up,
shining forth with triumph call
bestowing the glory

of He who came to save.
Millennium reign at Saviour's charge,
one thousand years passed like yesteryear,
though the grating of this pit's beasts
remained the same,
no rest,
we weary beaten forever slain.

The pit of darkened Hades opened
our judgement hour approacheth
for this we did again ascend
our sentence fore born known:
the second death.

I stood; alone accountable,
responsible in rags full mired.
His bright countenance shone eternal
my knees did bow
my eyes not raised,
ashamed,
dejected,
forsaken.
His book brought forth
my page His thumbnail opened,
in courtroom scene He gleaned the facts
no words He needed spoken,
He bid me plead
I said no need
for I knew His law was broken.

He said some fought,
some loudly screamed
some roared with indignation,
some bargained keen with riches lost
others earthly titled pleaded

some ambitious wrestled,
some with obsequious flattery contended
some too like me just silent stood
fate sealed by soon closed pages
white throne judgement ceased,
all mutterings ended.

Sentenced to burn in bowl flame red,
discarded to brimstone cauldron.
Hot roast flame that burns without destroy,
smoke cough, choke thick but yet still breathe,
gnashed chaff teeth worn thin
confined to a time of never ending.

I was summarily catapulted out of Majesty's sight,
again limbs flailed toward my fate;
my last vision, His laundered light bright back
a last glimpse as he turned again toward His children.
My screams echoed through eternity,
then blasted off bedroom wall
as I awoke,
startled,
fearful,
shaking full vigour.
Tears of understood mercy poured,
soaking pillow already drenched.
My confidence and vain ambitions shattered,
my past set aside for decay,
I must change.

There are no last rites for unrepentant breath,
to die less hope even worse than death.
Lost forever from He in life
they did so foolishly despise.

SELF CAST DOWN

1 Peter 5:6-7

"Therefore humble yourselves under the mighty hand of God,
that He may exalt you in due time,
casting all your care upon Him, for He cares for you."

I ran, I did stumble,
from Love I did flee,
pursued to the end
the Lord followed me.
My path was curved winding
bare rock at my feet,
cut, thorn sore, haggard,
ere soon I was beat.

Journeyed dark both mind and body
black depression buried deep,
not thinking clearly
wandering aimless foreboding streets.
Heart barely breathing,
deceived to the core,
brought to the knife edge
my life said no more.

Picked up the Lord's Word
pages made me think,
one path to destruction
another promised life.
But I battled, I wrestled
resistance hung tight,

like Jacob confronting Love
I fought with much might.

Ventured to battle, blood lust recharged,
gnashing of teeth, cavalry charge,
sword shaped sabre, I cut and I thrust
gained my advantage with hostile assault.
Blade run through, my enemy, He me defeated
I lay down my arms, white flag pleaded,
arbitration sought which He bought on the Cross
my ego was slain, cast down in dirt.

Pulse slowed down,
eternity stood still.
I either follow my self
else submit to His will.

THE SELF SERVING PRAYER

Matthew 6:5.

"And when you pray, you shall not be like the hypocrites.
For they love to pray standing in the synagogues and on the corners
of the streets, that they may be seen by men.
Assuredly, I say to you, they have their reward."

It can take a lifetime to surrender.

Then we lift our hands in praise and prayer.
A fragile human steeple
subjugated to majesty
whilst groaning for a promised blessing.
Intention pure,
yet still not too distant from manipulative intent.......

THE LAST TESTAMENT OF PONTIUS PILATE

Mark 15:15.

"So Pilate, wanting to gratify the crowd, released Barabbas to them; and he delivered Jesus after he had scourged Him, to be crucified."

I fear: I tremble at the memory.

I stand twice dead.
Circumstances prevailed.
Judgement has passed,
one from which I cannot flee.
Death clings
and its grasping shadow calls my name.
They came with obsequious bow
yet cursed this Tribune from within.

I fear: I tremble at the treachery.

Crucify Him! Crucify Him!
They roar and spit with poisoned breath.
Crucify Him! Crucify Him!
Their dark shroud like cancer spread.
Crucify Him! Crucify Him!
The baying of beasts; their cruel intent.
Crucify Him! Crucify Him!
I despise, yet I yield to their consent.

I fear: I tremble at the thought.

Can innocence and justice consort with ambitious hands?
Noble thought should commit to righteous deed.
Our frail life vapour expires
while the avarice of our lusts rises untiring.
The Elysium I manoeuvred my time toward
is now exposed as fraud.
The empire of this life short
but His reign will never end.

His eyes. They gazed with a light I cannot attain.
Are we not all Barabbas?

I fear: I tremble in my weakness.

Part 2

A great light shone forth

DESPERATION CRY

Luke 19:8-9

"Then Zacchaeus stood and said to the Lord,
"look, Lord, I give half of my goods to the poor; and if I have taken
anything from anyone by false accusation I restore fourfold."
And Jesus said to him, "Today salvation has come to this house,
because he also is a son of Abraham;
for the Son of Man has come to seek and to save that which was lost."

This vain palace,
world of subterfuge, poison chalice,
North Star compass upon rich man's tide.
Walked over people
their image cut to size,
they captivated by shadow of mind.
Secure in position
crowned by deceit and lies,
designed by I to entrap; to beguile.
In my growing comfort
I pillaged their souls,
anchor of workingman's silver
and royal shining gold.
This path I had chosen
rejoiced in full gain,
others gasping in wonder
mere mention my name.
Courted by majesty, by princes and kings,
ambassadors, embassies and glittering things,
stage at my beckon

wind sail at my back,
but suddenly, with no expectation
my journey turned black.
Nebuchadnezzar death shadow brought his attack
to my name, my riches,
to all I could spend,
vanity brought to narcissist's end.
Kin that once bowed now turned their back
inner chambers now sealed, my-self worth ransacked,
sanctuary of monarchs, sunburnt dry bone;
reflected now I upon deeds said and done
destroyed by myself by mercenary tongue.
Despite all my efforts to vain clear my name,
time took on character, played fickle dance game.
Cauldron bowl,
pyre funeral flame,
apologies not vast enough
forked tongue shifting blame.
Self cast down, guilty, ashamed,
despondent, afflicted, tears I did spend,
confronted by death
I contemplated self-end.
Screaming loud voices tormented my brain,
dry breath, red eyes, pulse slowed to descend.
There is no end to ceaseless grief,
no words of comfort at counsel speak,
black hole despair, dark tunnel of chaos,
skeletal shadow; life hope but lost.
In desperation cry
I roared the Lord's Prayer,
measured the words
felt His presence draw near.
Like Paul to Damascus,
I heard His still voice,
not discerned in the clamour

but with death point near passed.
My mind soothed now,
heart breath, soft quiet,
I basked in Christ's glory,
bathed in light.

The world wasn't big enough
for this Xanadu man,
the battles, the skirmishes of conquering hand.
All had been lost, but all to my gain
awakened now, quickened,
Christ Jesus enthroned:
it took salvation's sought scream
to taste of Love's gold.

QUICKENING

Colossians 1:19-20

"For it pleased the Father that in Him all the fullness should dwell,
and by Him to reconcile all things to Himself, by Him,
whether things on earth or things in heaven,
having made peace through the blood of His cross."

But small, it fell to strike upon Robin's breast,
this blood drop rivulet the size of faith burst mustard-seed.
Directing the imagination of history's courts,
more powerful than triumphant armies ten thousand strong,
prophesising heavenly dispensations across the decrees of lesser men.

But small, it fell to rest upon Robin's breast,
brown feather sentinel crying impassioned lament of Calvary birdsong.
Creation's reminder of beauty surveying tumult's bruise,
heart rhythm of hope in a dying world of anguish and grief.

But small, it took flight upon Robin's breast,
departing the caverns of Arimathea's rest, full witness to martyr's cheer.
Leaving city later sacked by Titus' gentile rage,
bearing testimony to where many did flee,
sharing their plight, their scorn, their Diaspora but promising later return.

But small, it fell again to strike my death,
I too must hark and fly to herald His coming throne.
The Son of Man's Blood has blotted out my sin,
my crimson flight and shout of ardent roar; I too will live for evermore.

HIS MIRACLE BROUGHT FORTH

Genesis 2:7.

"And the Lord God formed man of the dust of the ground
and breathed into his nostrils the breath of life,
and man became a living being."

Ruach.
God's breath of life.
My bent broken frame standing again.

Ruach.
The Spirit of God.
New beat to my heart; pulse getting strong.

Ruach.
The lifeblood of God.
New air in my lungs; new song to be sung.

Ruach.
The peace of God.
New joy in my steps as I walk along.

Ruach.
The fortitude of God.
New strength in my mind renewing thoughts one by one.

Ruach.
The cleansing of God.
New words in my mouth; old ways now gone.

Ruach.
The grace of God.
Now still in my heart; to Him I bow down.

Ruach.
The love of God.
New eyes to see; His cross is for everyone.

Ruach.
The cross of Jesus Christ.
God forgave my sin, for me He atoned.

Ruach.
The mercy of God.
New hope in my work; His deeds to be done.

Ruach.
The image of God.
His future is mine, to eternity I am bound.

THE WAY, THE TRUTH & THE LIFE

John 14:6

"Jesus said to him, "I am the way, the truth, and the life.
No one comes to the Father except through Me."

I endeavoured to discern direction,
to build my own way home;
venturing upon a broad gate
found carved upon ground of stone.
Pathway dangerous,
I slipped upon my feet,
knocking secret codes on doorways
down dark and shadowed streets.
Carnivals, dice rooms, racetracks, dance halls,
attractions in neon
flashing glimmer like jewels.
The end was deception,
prodigal coin haughtily spent,
allure then locked from inside
heralding quickly my own descent.
Stared I down the barrel of shotgun and of syringe,
I tried to find my succour in malcontent's dream,
glory days thought over
I feasted full on crumbs,
heartbeat near still,
my conscience clawed numb.
Falsehood friend and perished idols,
vain pleasure was all I found,
I bartered my future, my lifeblood nearly sold,
always seeking more
on the roads thought paved with gold.

Unexpectedly mid-October
a knock upon my heart,
the call of God upon my frame,
this life now set apart.
Delivered from the chaos
to His words upon a page,
brought by hand to narrow gate
to a new abundant land.
The testimony of pages my interest piqued and grew,
some words new, some refreshed others already knew.
But quickened in my Spirit
by Calvary's blood spilt nail,
The Lord stood me on firm rock,
on foundation bought by grace.
I AM the way, the truth and the life,
His direction pointed home.
Great light shone upon my face
His steps I just need follow,
His radiant love, a joy of heart
new pace to strengthening marrow.
He asked me pray, He bid me sing
to share my new found vigour,
I spoke new life when around was death
With joyful incantation,
I knocked on doors, called in the streets
putting end to world's temptation.
Christ alone, Christ alive,
through resurrection He is risen,
enthroned on high, the way, the life
by His truth my sins forgiven.

Fear not the author of your life,
bow before His Kingly reign,
allow His grace to still your heart
His truth to bring salvation.

DAMASCUS SUN

Acts of the Apostles 9:3.

*"As he journeyed he came near Damascus,
and suddenly a light shone around him from heaven."*

Punishing hot, horse dust roar,
murderous rage of plotting sword.
Kill those who believe, destroy the Cross,
through townland and village, burning crops.
Scything fodder like harvest corn,
frenzied citizens; bereft, forlorn.
Savage intentions of desperate men,
under the burn
of Damascus sun.

At the fore, Tarsus Saul,
mighty leader, Pharisee sworn;
learned in words and the wisdom of men,
satan's ambassador of hate's domain.
Catching breath, clasping whip and reins,
forced fixed mind to kill again;
serving his own god of blood and gore
under the burn
of Damascus sun.

Blinding light by Saviour's hand,
vainglorious life on sinking sand;
Saul unyoked from the path of man,
commissioned out of mortality for salvation's plan.
Ambition crushed yet not forsaken,

changed eternal, a new creation:
clothed in God's armour, new hope Paul found,
under the burn
of Damascus Sun.

I COST HIS BLOOD

Isaiah 53:5-6

*"But He was wounded for our transgressions; He was bruised for our iniquities;
The chastisement for our peace was upon Him, and by His stripes we are healed.
All we like sheep have gone astray; we have turned, everyone, to his own way;
and the Lord has laid on Him the iniquity of us all."*

Strongmen held the nation politicked the sway, cloven mercenaries shaded grey.
Weaving, scheming traditions of man, hidden corridors dark shake of hand.
They watched the law with pinching zeal, citizenry brought to deceiving heel,
bolstering wealth, retaining power, directing troops from high gilded tower.
The Son of Man He came to save; now God Himself stood in their way.
Incite the Romans, enflame the crowd; bait the rabble with voices loud,
against the King they did conspire; Judas the link; embezzler and liar.
There are two sides to a silver coin: victim's plight and betrayer's guile.

Memorial bread, reminding wine, betrayer's tongue with Judas spying.
Walk to garden, Gethsemane's keep, Christ Jesus to pray His fishermen to sleep
kneeling down by knotted tree, face down tears washed His earnest plea,
pressure wrestle, sweat charged man submitted to death for salvation's plan.
No Bethlehem star in faint low light, He stood his ground resisting flight
soldier's spear brought to test, knives sharpened held poised for death.
Judas sated with bursting purse, soldier's step echo with jibe and curse,
taunting, goading with prodding push, seeking reason to unleash bloodlust.

Chaos edge in cauldron bowl, heaving orchestrations of plotter's roar,
leaders clamour false witness sought, events converge circumventing truth.
Rulers without power cast off their cloaks, Rome's authority for death a must,
Lamb without blemish to Pilate went, no fault found to Herod sent.

Killer of John sat brazen and defiant, Jesus ignoring threat sat silent.
A washing of hands, Barabbas freed, Rome handed Christ over to Pharisees.
Beaten sore with briar sharp sticks, whips of bone with metal bits,
scourging mockers casting lots, King robed in purple with crown a top.

Slow plod walk through city gates, Calvary's cursed death ground,
the ragged man he stumbled fell, each laboured step bravely found.
Pounding hammer of grunt groan nails, shudder of bone and tearing of veins,
rope hoist to timber frame moan, His cross dropped quick in foundation hole.
"Call for Angels," came hate filled roar, some turned away others thirsted more,
thieves at each side one dark one light, promise to one Paradise that night.
His Blood flowed down a wooden cross full punishment for my sin he took,
when rejecting Father turned His back, my Lord and Saviour drew last breath.

Dark brooding sky, thunder scream, earthquake like lightening attack,
veil of temple was rent in two, Centurion stood still; awestruck.
From virgin's womb to virgin tomb His dead lifeless form laid down,
His Spirit departed to Abraham's bosom, the righteous of old went home.
Three days later Resurrection day, tombs circular stone rolled back,
His grave found empty, Christ Jesus arisen the King had forever beaten death.
All nations, all peoples through centuries time, by grace their sins atoned,
by His Blood He shed on Calvary's tree for the wretch, the sinner; I one.

ATONEMENT

1 Corinthians 1:18.

"For the message of the cross is foolishness to those who are perishing, but to us who are being saved it is the power of God."

The wearied withered brow of broken man
his winter's past reliving time again,
on face lined wretched, toiled and tasked
a day that dawns brings thoughts and shame unmasked.

His heart lies heavy clawing deep within
with blood that slows before its course begins
ten rugged steps to climb with sighing breath
one hundred voices follow dark as death.

The stain of scarlet moaning in this man
no path it finds, no release designed by human hand
no place to turn but cry with pleading eyes
reach out to Love that never once despised.

This life of sorrows lasts but just a day
with reapers scythe heralding quick to claim his pay.
However long you cry from bended knee,
grace is not folly; atonement must be believed.

GUILT EXPUNGED

Hebrews 9:27-28.

"And it is appointed for men to die once, but after this the judgement,
so Christ was offered once to bear the sins of many.
To those who eagerly wait for Him He will appear a second time apart from sin,
for salvation."

A sombre tension building
screamed between the courtroom walls,
The Judge sat upon His throne
prosecutor, aggressive,
argued heavy in his tone.
One corner clothed in venom
in a suit of fear and black,
took the floor enflamed and harried
to launch with stinged attack.
This falsehood thief malinger
in vague theory specialised,
his objective to fill the proceedings
with hate, deceit and lies.
The Judge loved truth and reason
righteousness undefiled,
a Holy Law would test each case
Book of Life at Majesty's side.
Revered and clothed in brightness,
compassion bathed in light,
He would listen with attention
bringing justice those contrite.

The snake shouted from the floor
reemed off crimes one by one,
seeking full death sentence
for the sins the charged had done.
The prosecutor experienced
by memory knew the facts,
times and dates with records
memories exacted from the past.
Murder in the thought-frame,
adultery done full blast,
coveting his neighbour,
his charge sheet skilfully pressed.
With bite forked tongue,
boom voice that did not quiver,
obsequious words of flattery
his bleak intention was delivered,
and when his case was argued
the sentence he did not fudge,
for the defendant he sought out hell
then sat and sneered the Judge.

The Throne gave nare a tremble
to the charges he paid no heed,
He turned to face the defendant
beckoned him to come and plead.
The room grew still and silent
crowd shifted in their seats
excitement palpable and heightened
all wondered who'd succeed.
Defendant stood, walked slowly
and bowed before the Judge,
turned his back to the prosecutor
made ready to tell the truth.
He looked around the courtroom
surveyed the seated from the stand,
took lung full air, said silent prayer
began his case to plead.

"As far from east to west
no blemish can be found,
search again from north to south
you'll see my claim is sound.
I used to be a liar
a narcissistic thief,
searching out my own advantage
never contemplating defeat.
I've said and done with vengeance
all the charges he outlined,
But there came a day
change came my way
a day to be reborn.
I tell the truth for I will not lie
by grace my sins are gone.
I learnt about a Saviour
God and man from heaven sent,
He lived, then died,
was raised again, forever beating death.
He did it for the sinner
for those by His blood repent,
for the murderer, the harlot
the broken and the spent.
You see I repented long ago
of the things he said I've done,
I'm trusting in my Saviour
in God's only begotten Son.
Though now my days are over
the earth I've bid farewell,
I stand alone afore you
pleading mercy through Christ's Blood."

The audience sat enraptured,
the testifier did advocate,
the prosecutor squirmed uneasily
knowing well the defendant's fate.

The Judge stood ever silent
and leaving Kingly throne
He placed His hand on the defendant's back
and embraced him near to hug.
Like long lost friends united
He placed His mouth to ear,
and speaking firm but slowly
we all leaned in to hear.
"I've listened to your story
rejoiced at end of tale,
I welcome all my children
who trust in My Son's name.
You cannot earn your place here
it is My gift through faith,
for none shall boast on entry
through Heaven's celestial gate."
He turned with pointed finger
the snake trembled then recoiled,
"begone thou vagabond disputer
for you your case is spoiled,
you contortor of morbid confusion
I've listened every word,
I have here My own conclusion
My verdict to be heard."

The gavel pounded heavily
wood echo sounded round,
The Saviour's grace has goodly triumphed,
unmerited grace shall now abound.

"Case dismissed
Guilt expunged."

Next...

(Your turn. What will you say?)

PSALM 70 TIMES 7

Mark 8:34.

"When He had called the people to Himself, with His disciples also,
He said to them,
"Whoever desires to come after Me,
let him deny himself and take up his cross, and follow Me."

Seventy times seven,
I fell again.
Is there any hope left?
I want to please my Father,
it is my fervent desire:
yet when I slip am I beyond repair?
I walk then offend again.
But this life I must live by faith in Jesus Christ
and not by my own performance.

He leads me and teaches me His way
and I slowly learn,
to recognise sin
and to wage a mighty war against it
and then by grace alone leave it behind.

Lethargy and coldness of heart
oft times befriend me
to replace joy and love as my companions.
It is these times I need repent
and read His Word.
I will listen to his soft still voice
that quietly urges me on to follow.

Part 2: A great light shone forth

I must pick up and carry my cross
to follow again.

Seventy times seven
I fell again.
But there is hope.......

IN CONVERSATION

<u>John 10:10</u>

The thief does not come except to steal, and to kill, and to destroy.
I have come that they may have life,
and that they may have it more abundantly.

"Tomorrow, a day closer to death, for your life passeth like a vapour.
Tomorrow, when the sins of yesterday becometh the judgement of today.
When bride becometh a widow,
where orphan hood passeth to unsuspecting child;
all will be lost in a decaying history of human misery and toil.

Vigour gone.
Dreams vanished.
Hope vanquished.
Gone the hissing heat of argument.
Dead the striving of wilful covetousness.
Lost the lustful gaze of youthful intent.

What say ye now men of wisdom?
What ambitious intent remaineth?
Where rest ye now as I satan creepeth the earth?
For I beckoneth for thine flesh,
My seductive lips desireth thine soul,
your very life I claimeth as ye struggle all with malicious vanity.......
Come now. Play my merry dance......"

"AWAY!
That child ist mine," roareth the Majesty of Judah.
"Away thou scornful fiend.
AWAY!

Plough thy path to damnation yet leavest thou mine child.
Mine ransomed pearl.
Mine precious stone.
Mine fruitful bounty.
Begone thou crimson tempter.
Begone thou snake of frenzy.
Begone thou beast of Eden for that child ist mine.
Bought by blood mine child is redeemeth.

My peace; it passeth all understanding.
My love; it covers a multitude of sins.
My life; it redeemeth and reconcileth.
My hope; is it not an eternal bounty?
Away thou fiend of murderous rage and folly,
for that child ist mine.
AWAY."

HIS CHANGE WROUGHT FORTH

The Acts of the Apostles 4:12

"Nor is there salvation in any other,
for there is no other name under heaven given among men
by which we must be saved."

A light from Heaven
struck He upon my breast,
my frame but weak
He doth me quiet arrest.

A sound from Heaven
leathward a trumpet call,
singular upon me
He doth this time me enthral.

A voice from Heaven
stillness of heart I so discern,
a weight lifteth from the sense
He doth not me spurn.

His Word from Heaven
impress to burn my spirit so,
meditate now upon the mind
He doth me inward change.

A call from Heaven
venture hence across the land,
He sheltereth me now
He doth me lead by hand.

His life from Heaven
His Blood He alone shed forth,
flow mingled down
He doth from tree cut hewn.

My citizenship now in Heaven
by grace my sin He did expunge,
my home eternal
He doth for me prepare.

My heart with Spirit filled joy
rejoiceth now, at rest at last in peace.

Part 3

Confident and assurred

WHAT BEAUTY

Ephesians 2:8.

*"For by grace you have been saved through faith,
and that not of yourselves; it is the gift of God,
not of works, lest anyone should boast."*

But dust the splendours of this globe,
there is another we declare our home,
the heavenly realm for us The Master did establish,
barrage of stars, full light, announces forth His name.
Here an hour we must abate then time pass mourn,
this creation groaning seeking world of evermore.

I set my sight toward a time of no tomorrows,
weary, wrinkle tale my shadow frame will tell.
But yet rejoice,
no last breath sorrow,
He will forever claim me home;
carry me that place with hand that bled with nail.

If you are tired, bent beat with rigour toil,
fret not child His calm will softly still your storm.
A choir full sing His exultation,
streets of golden jewel, alive for you to roam.

In this life we race to meet our heroes
then observe vain frailty of human weakened bone,
rise up your heart,
your eyes toward salvation,
what beauty rests,
confident in Him alone.

An inexpressible beauty manifest in your tomorrow,
no death can cry midst your frail decay,
there is a place for you forgiven sinner
where you can rest with joy in Holy Name.
The tide now creeks upon the harbour,
faint light now brings me soon to pass,
I shall not fret nor anger at my passing,
no fear I feel as I hold tight upon new life.

Hark herald voice bring joy of His salvation.
Hark herald rest, His grace for evermore.
Hark herald shout His name with righteous exaltation.
Hark herald sing; Christ's name, Eternal Love.

HIS NAME ALONE

1 Timothy 2:5.

"For there is one God and one Mediator between God and men, the Man Christ Jesus."

Not by church,
not by steeple,
by denomination
or priestly people.
Not by ceremony
Or doing good,
living right
or balancing books,
pope's crozier
or preacher's soar,
you are saved by
His Name alone.

Not by flesh
nor idols stone,
not by silver
or shining gold.
Not by coin
or banker's note,
you are saved by
His Name alone.

Not by hate
or false forced love,
not by pomp
nor circumstance,

boasting pride
or one up game,
only by
His Holy Name.

Not by address
earthly vain,
power, position
or passing fame.
Furnished home
or type of car,
education, books,
graduation scroll,
you are saved by
His name alone.

Not by strength
strongman's roar,
not by cajoling
or works of law.
Accountant's zeal
or penny pinching,
doing works
or even helping.
Animal sacrifice
nor sun or moon
you are saved by
His Name alone.

Not by sport
by running man,
kicker of ball
or boxing match.
Not by singer
by favourite band,

spinning single
all sinking sand.
But in that place
the heavenly realm,
we will worship
His Name alone.

Not by politic
or human leader,
prince or potentate
or monarch king.
Not by minister
or company icon
human fraternity
or brotherhood of man.
You are saved by grace
through faith in Christ,
all sufficient
He paid full price.
He gave His life
so trust in Him,
you are saved by
His Name alone.

All things can be good
likewise bad,
some ruler's bring peace
others distil sad.
We suffer distraction
yet can't evade time,
so enjoy your life
and live with joy,
then on that day
when He calls you home,
stand firm upon
His Name alone.

HARD TRUTH

Matthew 7:13-14.

"Enter by the narrow gate
for wide is the gate and broad is the way that leads to destruction,
and there are many who go in by it.
Because narrow is the gate and difficult is the way which leads to life,
and there are few who find it."

The stars fell from the sky;
Orion, Centaurus, Perseus now melted, collapsed and void.
A black sun cast an insipid dullness
across a dark land.
A vague shadowy light bringing forth a day of
destruction, doom and judgement.

The dead walked slow and dishevelled,
treading toward gallows
shearing silence towards fire and decay.
Townland and communities.
Families, parents and children,
designed for righteousness
but lost in a web of ungracious conceit and avarice.
Life course plotted in defiance, indignation and ignorance.
Parents, given responsibility for their offspring,
choosing for their charges not life
but rather the dungeons of death.

The righteous did not remain unscathed.
Their testimony bore a tale of persecution and despair.
They witnessed their own venture blindingly forth
toward a future covenanted annihilation,
their earnest pleas abhorred and scorned.
They were also murdered in their millions;
racked, broken and bent misshapen.
Even their God and Judge it seemed turned His back;
they suffering brutal but loving chastisement.
Hammer blow against anvil shaping them into the
image of Him who was crucified for their sins.
Yet their unquenched hope remained the New Jerusalem,
undiminished and shining forth in all the surrounding bleakness.

Sheep and Goat.
Wheat and tare.
Together but separated that day,
the day when time ran out.

DISCERNMENT

The Book of Proverbs 3:5-6.

"Trust in the Lord with all your heart and lean not on your own understanding;
In all your ways acknowledge Him,
and He shall direct your paths."

To understand character,
listen as if you cannot see,
watch as if you cannot hear.

Then.......

You will have compassion on the many
and be wise of the few.

BE YE NOT DECEIVED

James 4:7

*"Therefore submit to God.
Resist the devil and he will flee from you."*

From measured distance,
I spied a thief: a liar.

They travelled fast and light
upon that cold dark morn
securing a steady pace,
cresting hillock then forest thicket;
the rider's exhaled breath leaving a clouded ghostlike mist in its wake.

He was preceded by carrion feasting, fat, bountiful ravens.
Three score and six obsidian heralds of death.
Red eyed beasts,
announcing the impending arrival
of the enemy himself: satan,
ruler of the kingdom of men and the fallen sons of hell.

At heel, six rasping stalking dark grey wolves
instructed to rip and tear,
sinew and muscle careering forward toward spiritual carnage.
Their prey: one soul of man,
one doomed to sudden and overdue destruction.

Silhouetted against that bleak morn I also observed
six large coal black plumed horses
strapped in cold leather,
their shining buckles like chains

fashioned for men
that swing unknowingly over the abyss.
Reins and whip jerking viciously by shadowed rider,
he shrouded in stench and putrid brutality.
Cavernous eyes surveying land and humble domain,
ploughed field and furrow, sweeping riverbank meander.
Careful intent not to pass his claim
but rigorous in ferocity and zeal.

This demonic troupe pulled a darkened hearse,
a stark, glass fronted four wheeled creaking crypt,
hinged door awaiting yet another unsuspecting guest.
Baying nostril steam,
jousting hooves,
neighing fury,
foaming spittle,
halting now;
clamouring for prize.
The heightened anxiousness of restless beasts
culminating in the sickening silence of one stretched second.

To my unexpected surprise they terminated outside my abode,
his words penetrating my ear now stuck heavy to the door.

"The best of my ambush,
the very wickedness and unparalleled joy of my deceit
is to catch them unawares," he said in raised voice directed to scare.
"Then when they realise that I am outside a
gentle knock upon lintel frame is best to terrify,
to arrest,
to hesitate a last cry for mercy.
Some with curious indignation wrestle,
alas to my merriment, their misadventure soon overtakes.
Witness......
a forlorn stare,
a tremble,

the lightest quiver of lips,
dry parched skin,
mixed with resigned forbearance.
Full knowledge of unrighteous deed
portrayed in fear and sometimes odour,
caught timeless and forever in a wretched sin clenched face.
They are mine.
Altogether mine."

"The door always opens,
no lock can prevail.
It is only then that I, their master, enter;
never a need for formal announcement."

"Come now, it's time," his voice gaining a hurried anticipation.
"The truth I have distorted from the beginning
from the eyes and minds of lustful man.
I that have deceived through the ages
plot now your soon demise.
Your life is mine,
your next breath I must now collect.
My foolish, deluded, vainglorious bonded slave;
in life you denied my reign,
death now will help you think."

"Come now! Its time," he now excited by fevered expectation.
"My hounds desire your rancid carcass.
We leave now for eternity,
come now, come hither;
join the already resident souls of the damned." ......

A gentle knock came upon my framed entrance:
the accompanying echo charged forth to suck all hope.
My ticking mantle clock extending life,
the hammer hand of time passing noisily second by second.

Tick,
Tock.

Tick,
Tock.

Tick,
Tock.

Tick,
Tock.

Tick,
Tock.

A loud, demanding, expectant roar ensued,
"What ails thee?
Where is thine haste?
The darkness awaits.
Come!" ......

.......Composed.
I decided to answer.
Calm and confident I lifted farmhouse latch,
steady resolve to watch him flee.
With no fear I launched forth.

"Care not I for your circus of death,
conjured smoke and wolf raven flesh.
Fraudulent undertaker's travelling grave;
dare you stand here, unrighteous knave.
Despoiler of nations and empires long vanished,
Truth be known your reign has been vanquished.
Countenance faltering?
Confidence extinguished?

Words failing now?
Your work here is finished.
Thrice exposed in wilderness sand,
Let your shadow again fall by my Saviour's hand.

Be ye not deceived.

God, as you know, took on our frame,
Christ Jesus Himself born as a babe,
to extinguish our sins,
He coming to save.
Repent He declared,
My Kingdom is at hand,
preaching and healing
across His covenanted but hungry land.

Be ye not deceived.

I am the way, the truth and the life He decreed,
our only gracious mediator fulfilling our need.
Rejected, despised and chastised by men
satisfying prophecy again and again.
Broken, beaten, tattered and torn
crucified on a cross spilling His Blood for our scorn.
You thought it over when He died on that tree
but that work was not finished as you now see.

Be ye not deceived.

Buried three days
the good news unfolded.
The tomb was found empty
the Risen Christ had departed.
His resurrection confirmed
He left us His Spirit,

by the Father's right hand
He now executes judgement.

For by grace we are saved
not by works lest we boast.
I am bought at great price
your lies and vice exposed."

I held no pity for this miserable creature
his face contorted, frame bent and pulled asunder.
No mercy for this fiend
whose currency is death and murder.
He turned and fled through yonder gate
spilling his chalice of poisoned hate.
I watched him leave
past the first glistening of dewy sunlight,
past the sleepy humming and scratchy foraging
of bird and country crawler.
His wide eyed retinue surprised yet fearful,
it would this day be a darker stay in Hades;
his false authority to be re-established.
Usurped not by royal Prince or noble Knight
but by a simple Blood bought potato farmer:
a man of pure motive and Spirit-filled intent.

Likewise much loved reader,
Be ye not deceived.
Expect such a visit
for it will soon unawares come.

Repent and believe in Him who alone ransomed you by His Blood.
Though He died, He now is alive: risen.
Then upon that day and without hesitation,
exercise your God given sword sharpened authority without trepidation.

ETERNITY

Jeremiah 29:11

"For I know the thoughts that I think toward you, says the Lord,
thoughts of peace and not of evil,
to give you a future and a hope."

Most people form themselves to this world.
This Babylon:
where moth and rust collide.

Some images exist on scroll, plinth or canvass.
These idols of imagination reside in an imperfect transience.

Some people are created for Eternity.
Some things are just so.

"Why you ask?"…….

Because that work is beautiful.

You can lose this world or you can lose everything.

THE PRAYER

Matthew 6:9-13.

"In this manner; therefore pray:
Our Father in heaven, Hallowed be Your name.
Your kingdom come.
Your will be done on earth as it is in heaven.
Give us this day our daily bread.
And forgive us our debts, as we forgive our debtors.
And do not lead us into temptation,
But deliver us from the evil one.
For Yours is the kingdom and the power and the glory forever."
Amen.

It does take a lifetime to surrender.

And when the Holy Spirit's work is underway
we lift our hands and say.......

"Thy will be done."

PRAISE HIS HOLY NAME

The Revelation of Jesus Christ 21:3-4.

"And I heard a loud voice from heaven saying,
"Behold the tabernacle of God is with men, and He will dwell with them,
and they shall be His people.
God Himself will be with them and be their God.
And God will wipe away every tear from their eyes;
there shall be no more death, nor sorrow, nor crying.
There shall be no more pain, for the former things have passed away."

Praise His Holy Name.

His light permeates and radiates the Heavenly realm,
His majesty enthroned on high.
Father, Son and Holy Spirit in oneness declare
Let Us again live in the midst of our children.

Hark the timbrels and instruments of His domain;
strings and wind bellows, none devised by human hand.
Notes, sweet with music never heard on the old now passed earth,
orchestrations of beauty and delight.
Sounds and melodies that mere word cannot describe,
living movement, living joy, living Love.

His congregation of Heaven gathered.
Those who worshiped from thousands of years ago
joined with peoples from the more recent hundreds,
together with those caught up, those martyred of old and new.

This heavenly choir of love and praise,
all nations, all tongues, peoples from every tribe,
crowns cast aside in humility, reverence and thanksgiving.
Voices pressed together; His bride in timeless eternity.

Praise the Father, the Son Christ Jesus and The Holy Spirit.
Praise Him for His death, His atoning Blood and His resurrection.
Praise Him for the forgiveness of sin and for eternal life.
Praise Him for His mercy and His great love.
Praise Him for His free gift of sovereign grace,
not earned by works lest any man should boast.

Praise His Holy Name.

Zechariah 14:9.

"And the Lord shall be King over all the earth.

In that day it shall be –

"The Lord is one,"

And His name one."

The last words of Redmond Holt…

"I am a man of no importance or consequence. I would like to be remembered as a man who loved his children and as a man who was a loyal and faithful friend to the few who opened their hearts and homes to me."

Other books by Redmond Holt

dystHOPEia

Mammon

Eulogy: Jerusalem 70AD.

America

Are you inspired to write a book?

Contact

Maurice Wylie Media
Your Inspirational & Christian Book Publisher
Based in Northern Ireland, serving readers worldwide

www.MauriceWylieMedia.com

www.ingramcontent.com/pod-product-compliance
Lightning Source LLC
Chambersburg PA
CBHW041148110526
44590CB00027B/4166